THE ORGANIC CHURCH
VS
THE "NEW TESTAMENT" CHURCH

THE ORGANIC CHURCH
VS
THE "NEW TESTAMENT" CHURCH

Gene Edwards

SeedSowers Publishing
Jacksonville, Florida

The Organic Church vs the "New Testament" Church

Published by: SeedSowers Publishing
                  P.O. Box 3317, Jacksonville, FL 32206
                  800-228-2665
                  www.seedsowers.com

Edwards, Gene
The Organic Church vs the "New Testament" Church

ISBN 10: 0-9778033-1-7
ISBN 13: 978-0-9778033-1-6
1. House Church

Times New Roman 13pt

ALSO BY GENE EDWARDS

THE CHRONICLES OF HEAVEN
Christ Before Creation
The Beginning
The Escape
The Birth
The Triumph
The Return

THE FIRST-CENTURY DIARIES
The Silas Diary
The Titus Diary
The Timothy Diary
The Priscilla Diary
The Gaius Diary

INTRODUCTION TO THE DEEPER CHRISTIAN LIFE
Living by the Highest Life
The Secret to the Christian Life
The Inward Journey

Paul's Way of Training Workers or the Seminary's Way
The Shocking Story of the History of Bible Study
Why You Should Consider Leaving the Pastorate
The Organic Church vs the "New Testament" Church
Problems and Solutions in House Churches
How to Start a House Church from Scratch
Why So Many House Churches Fail and What to Do about It
The Christian Woman . . . Set Free
Beyond Radical
The Divine Romance
A Tale of Three Kings
The Prisoner in the Third Cell
Letters to a Devastated Christian
Exquisite Agony
Dear Lillian
Climb the Highest Mountain
Revolution, The Story of the Early Church
How to Meet in Homes
The Day I Was Crucified as Told by Jesus the Christ
Your Lord Is a Blue Collar Worker

TABLE
OF
CONTENTS

———•❖•———

INTRODUCTION

The entire world desperately needs either a New Testament church or an organic church. But which? The difference between the two is life or death.

The following words I heard even before I became a Christian:

"We must be New Testament." and/or "We need to return to a New Testament church."

Would not everyone agree with those statements?

Let us see. . . .

CHAPTER ONE

DARE WE CHALLENGE THIS INCONTESTABLE VIEW?

The truth is, there is no such thing as the "New Testament" church . . . not even in the New Testament! What the New Testament records is the story of the organic experiences of churches, from A.D. 30 to A.D. 70. We have a clear record of about a dozen churches in Century One. All these ekklesia were different and all were organic. We cannot re-create a New Testament church! But, if we dare, we can see the rebirth of an organic being—a woman, a living, breathing person—the ekklesia.

Attempting to bring about the rebirth of the ekklesia will fail if you use the verse-here-and-verse-there method. To do so is to end up having a static view of the ekklesia, whereas the organic church of Century One "felt her way along" from day to day.

By the way, I expect few men to understand this book in this generation. But the few who do will cause a future generation to see this as obvious.

CHAPTER TWO

WHAT IS IT THAT ASSEMBLES?

We often translate the Greek word *ekklesia* as assembly. But what is it that is being assembled? It is the assembling together of the living parts of Jesus Christ. That means His head *and* His many members. We picture this in a marriage, when the man and woman become united as one person.

It takes hard work to stop this lady *ekklesia* from being organic. It is her biological nature. It is only her organic function that can truly *restore the first-century church.* Men who try to build a church interfere with her beautiful organic nature.

Let us drop in on a group of men intent on ignoring biology but committed to verses pulled out of context. Here is what these men are thinking:

"We will need miracles. A New Testament church will have to have deacons and elders. There should be prophets, etc. Women should not talk in the meeting. And we will meet in a home."

These men then begin gathering up all these elements, and they believe "We now have a New Testament church."

No, forcing those elements into an organization does not make it a New Testament church, but Dr. Ludwig Frankenstein would be impressed. They have only one problem. What they have put together is dead. This approach does not produce a living creature. There is no place on earth more lifeless than a gathering of Christians in the house church movement when it has tried to reconstruct the elements of a New Testament church. The house church, their "New Testament" church, will be boredom itself . . . as great as the boredom they experienced in their previous Sunday morning church service.

There is no substitute for biology . . . and that includes bringing together an organization.

CHAPTER THREE

THE GENETICS OF LIFE

As a baby grows, so grows the ekklesia.

There is no such thing as a New Testament church; but there is a corporate living person, the bride of Christ. She is a *living* organism. She is also captive to the laws of genetics. As in genetics, there is an unstoppable pattern. That is, her ways, her nature, her expression are encoded in her. The only way such a beautiful woman will live again is to give her the chance to live out her encoded nature. Then she naturally becomes what she naturally is.

There are two choices: You can have a corpse or you can have the DNA of the church.

Consider the DNA of a baby, a human embryo, a human that has been conceived in a mother's womb. The parents, when they find that a child is on the way, do not fall down on their faces praying that the baby will have a nose, two ears, two eyes, ten fingers and ten toes. Without even consciously considering it, the parents know that inside that baby there is an encoded nature which will produce a human being. The baby grows by an irreversible, unstoppable biological pattern unique to humans. That child, to no one's surprise, will have toes, fingers, eyes, ears, and will look like a human, only smaller.

So, also, is the bride of Christ. She is a living being. She is born, and eventually she grows up to have organically all those elements an ekklesia is supposed to have which you find chronicled in the story . . . that is, if men do not interfere with her organic growth.

We are looking at biology versus a coroner's forensics!

We would think it strange if someone tried to have a baby by putting together different parts of the human body and then announcing, "Here is a baby!"

That is exactly what men do when they attempt to have a New Testament church. They read about what once was, and they begin attaching pieces together. Later they announce, "Ours is a church just like the church was long ago, after Pentecost." Sirs, you bypassed the birth and growth processes reserved exclusively by the Holy Spirit.

———— • ————

CHAPTER FOUR

THE SPONTANEOUS CHURCH

It may be a long time before the original nature of the church catches on among us frontal-lobe evangelicals; but, in the meantime, the spontaneous/ organic church is born everyday somewhere in the world. Just as certainly, everyday a spontaneous church is killed by someone who is making sure it is a "New Testament" church. That kills her nature, her DNA, her purity, her spontaneity and innocence. . . all in order to be "scriptural," when in fact, what comes out is not scriptural at all.

You can put together your deacons and your elders, plus whatever else you find in your scriptural view. You can gather up all those parts, but you will not end up with the *life* of the church.

That, dear reader, is exactly what you have when you have a *New Testament church.* All the parts, all the titles, the activities, yet you will not have life.

What you are attempting is biologically impossible. Essentially, you have what Ludwig had—a dead corpse— and, though you have all the parts, you have no electricity to give life. All the Bible study on earth will not produce life, nor will all the titles found in a New Testament concordance. Only biology produces life. You are up against the immutable laws of biology. Biology calls forth a child who has in its DNA a pattern. In this case, we speak of the biology that brings forth a living bride. Plus, understand, the church is not only a living entity, but there is a divine pattern woven into her very existence.

Somehow we get it in our minds that if we will preach and teach New Testament practices, we will in some way end up with a New Testament church.

See the contrast. God's divinity, God's life, God's pattern, God's DNA permeate the bride of Christ. We are dealing not only with DNA, but with the highest life in the universe.

Life is life, and the way that a church becomes a church is by setting free her DNA. She will find her inwrought course! Do that, plus add a great deal of time and a lot of Christ as her food, and she cannot but become what she is, the ekklesia!

The church, by becoming the church, has means given to her by her divine pattern, and she ends up being just what this world so desperately needs: an organic expression of Christ and His counterpart.

Has it ever occurred to you that in an organic body of believers, an elder is a biological result of life? Or that church planters, evangelists, etc. come out of her organic encoding? Put it another way: A corporate body of people living by divine life is the only way the bride of Christ comes into being. As sure as a baby produces a nose, a spontaneous organic church will produce elders, etc. When she is left alone to grow up, she produces, no, she *becomes* the ekklesia. But this cannot happen unless you leave her alone.

CHAPTER FIVE

PAUL'S WAYS WITH THE ORGANIC CHURCH

Instead of putting verses together to get a New Testament church, why have we not examined how Paul produced organic churches? Paul had a *way*. A biological girl can come into being when the church is raised up in a way not too dissimilar to Paul's way.

What was Paul's way? He raised up a church, helped it for a time, and *then he left* that lady the church on her own. (Is that ever in contrast to the way men do it today!) It is unlikely that you or I or anyone else is going to have an organic church if we do not employ Paul's way of planting churches. If a church is properly *spiritually equipped* (if she is Christ-centered: that is, if Christ is the center of her corporate experience), little by little she will begin to have the characteristics of the early churches which Paul raised up. She will display characteristics which men are now striving so hard to come up with but will *never* achieve by their usual efforts. Of course, they can produce a pastor, who today holds everything together while also producing a mute laity; but that is a far cry from Paul's way.

It is either biology's way or Ludwig's way.

The natural elements of the body of Christ arrive on the scene without using the methods employed by

Ludwig, M.D. The doctrinal speculations of man cannot come close to producing the wonders of the corporate birth and growth of life that is divine life.

This all boils down to one question: Do you trust laymen on their own? The answer of the ages is that ministers do not trust God's people on their own. That fact may be the underlying reason that men's version of a "New Testament" church keeps coming up with a pastor and a mute laity.

Without exception, all the churches that Paul planted in the gentile world were left alone; and, in every case, God's people managed to survive and express Christ and His church.

Could we but open our eyes and see what was going on in the book of Ephesians,* with its list of "the fivefold gifts," our present one-hundred-fifty-year-old understanding of this passage would change forever.

Let us dare do just that!

---

* Ephesians should probably actually be named Second Colossians. This letter was not referred to as the Ephesian letter until 400 A.D., and then it was misnamed!

CHAPTER SIX

A VILLAGE IN EASTERN ASIA MINOR

The letter to the Ephesians was not written to the church in Ephesus. It was written to the church in Colossae. That, in itself, changes everything. In this letter, Paul is writing to a group of Christians meeting in the home of a gentleman named Philemon; and Colossae is a village, not a metropolis, and is ninety miles east of Ephesus.

How do we come up with today's image of an *evangelist* as being in a metropolis, when the term was in reference to a group of people gathering in a village?

You can expect evangelists and all the "gifted ones" to grow up eventually out of the DNA of the gathering, even in the little village of Colossae. Expect to rewrite all your definitions of evangelist . . . *and* all the other gifts and offices on the list. Quoting the "five-fold gifts" in Ephesians (that is, Colossae), you would think that village had produced a tent evangelist with a worldwide ministry of evangelism, as well as a man who could tell you what you were thinking, an internationally-renowned Bible teacher, and a pulpiteer extraordinaire.

No, the evangelists were average brothers in the church, and the average person in Philemon's living room could not read!

Would you like to wade into this a little deeper?

The man who had raised up the church in Colossae was a man from this very village of Colossae; but as the letter was received, he was not present. He was in Rome, Italy with Paul and was ill. He had left the Colossae church (as a good church planter should). The letter which Paul wrote to the Colossians was intended to be delivered to the church in Colossae by the man who had raised up the church; but since he was too sick to travel, Paul chose another church planter, a man named Tychicus, to deliver the Colossian letter. Now, Tychicus was not from Colossae, but he was from Asia Minor; therefore, he spoke the same language as the people in Colossae. Tychicus traveled to Asia Minor and to Colossae. He read Paul's letter to the church in Colossae. Keep all that in mind as you read this letter which contains the part about the fivefold gifts.

These "towering" people with the gifts mentioned in Ephesians are in an obscure village in Colossae. Our vaulted descriptions of these gifted men lack reality when seen in the factual ekklesia in Colossae. Hearing us talk about these five gifts today, you would think the church planter, the prophet, the evangelist, teacher and pastor were people who had reached some pope-like status in the kingdom of God. Instead, they could all fit in Philemon's living room, in a tiny village where most people made their living raising sheep.

Not quite the dramatic practice we learn about today, is it? The great awesome idea of specially gifted men vanishes. (Churches today need drama because they do not have the reality of Christian community.) Colossae flies in the face of all our modern definitions of "special" people! When we face the fact that gifts did not make people special, the mystery of it all is lost, is it not?

CHAPTER SEVEN

ORGANIC DEFINITIONS OF THE GIFTS

One of the first things I did the first week I enrolled in the seminary was to read a book which defined all the major terms of the New Testament. This included the definition of a prophet, elder, healer, administrator, deacon, evangelist, etc.

In my observation of an organic ekklesia, on the other hand, I find that in the organic setting, a whole new world of definitions emerge; and all of them are far more comfortable, more realistic, and have more of the human touch, more believable, more attainable. In an organic church, the brothers and sisters who may have some gift will not look like the beautiful people you see on Christian television. Rather, the gifts they have look like they could be part of anyone's life. The church is local, and so are the gifted people. They come forth out of the matrix of a local gathering, and you will find these people disconcertingly *average*. They are not extraordinary people, but Christians doing what Christ's own body does. They *gradually* grew up in the life of the church.

When the body grows and develops its eyes, toes, fingers, etc., you may be astounded to discover that all your high-sounding definitions of elders, evangelists, prophets, and other gifted ones will have to change.

Such views are the result of long-time misunderstandings.

In a natural environment of growth, the so-called offices and gifts just surface, and they do not look so much like offices, nor do they look special. There is nothing awesome about gifted ones because they are all local, and they are all very ordinary people. These "gifted ones" grew up in the sight of everyone else. Their faults, weaknesses and ordinariness are known by all. This takes away from the spookiness of the mysterious specially-endowed gifted ones. (The elder or gifted brother is nothing more than the brother who lives next door.)

Ever hear the term, "We need to recover the five-fold gifts"? Well, you do not need to recover the five-fold gifts or any other gifts! All you need is church life. These gifts will emerge *organically*. But such church life is found in a Christ-centered church, not a minister-centered church, nor an elder-centered church, nor any "special person" church. The functioning of gifts becomes the ordinary experience of the body of the Lord Jesus Christ. Gifts are encoded in the nature, the DNA, of church life . . . which just does what it does because of the life that is intrinsic to it. This is the church. Everything else is manmade organization.

First let us look at the gift of healing.

CHAPTER EIGHT

HEALING

What about healing and healers?

Again, this is a local matter. Expect Christians who heal to be people operating simply in the confines of the *local* assembly. And that is all it is—a local function.

A church, after enough time to grow, will express itself with some gifts. A church will have healings! Healing is so common and so natural in the church's own locale, that it is really not all that dramatic.

Healing is one of the natural expressions of an organic church—natural and unheralded. Healing comes by means of unheralded people. Healing is not something that everyone jumps up and down and shouts about. It does not get an overdose of attention. Healing in the church is like breathing to the human body. Healing is part of the daily outliving of the body of Christ.

Almost disappointing, is it not?

Understand this, our era is simply not suited to employ properly the gifts and other functions that are necessary for a spontaneous, natural expression of the church—be they spiritual things or practical things.

CHAPTER NINE

PASTOR

Which brings us to the ubiquitous term *pastor* in the passage on gifts.

First of all, the word pastor does not appear in the New Testament. By the way, neither does its practice. The word is plural—not pastor, but pastors.

If there is anything which needs to be redefined, it is *pastor*. All over this planet, the word *pastor* immediately conjures up the image of a man standing in front of a mute people sitting in pews while he brings an oration behind a pulpit; and this he does *every* Sunday morning. Add to that: This man does this same routine year after year. No such man existed in Century One. He was not in Colossae, not in Philemon's house. When we look at the original meaning of the word pastors, we find the word refers to those who simply have *caring hearts* for the other people in the body of Christ— and they care for them. What would that mean for the people gathering in a village in Colossae? "Pastors" had no special position among God's people. They were certainly not running the church. They were nothing more than functioning members of the body of Christ.

A pastor is someone who cares, someone who comforts, someone who takes care of the brothers and sisters who have needs.

The gifts come forth out of the matrix of a local gathering. Pastors, as the other gifted members, are local people. You will find them disconcertingly *average*. They are not even extraordinary people, just Christians doing what Christ's own body does—local people who *gradually* grew up, and grew out of the life of the church.

And now we shall see that if gifted members hold offices, their offices are not forever.

—•—

CHAPTER TEN

ELDERS

You will find the following statement widely accepted, but it is organically not true: "Once an elder, always an elder." Paul possibly implies this is not true when he says, "It is a good thing for a man to seek being an elder." Do you realize that statement cannot be applied to the present-day practice of elders? Since eldership is considered to be *permanent,* you might say an elder's meeting is virtually hermetically sealed—you cannot get in! In view of Paul's statement, the poor soul who would want to "seek being an elder" (which is a good thing) will have to just sit and wait out his entire lifetime until some elders die.

Our observation: Elders should not be forever, because once in a while there is a man whom the church might see as an elder, but whom they would not look at that way five years later.

CHAPTER ELEVEN

DARE WE ORDAIN?

The Christian faith, from era to era, has lived on misconceptions, the pope being a prime example. One of today's is the near-dictatorial position of an elder. For that reason, I can think of nothing we could do to cause so much damage *and* destroy the freedom of a church as to openly give a man the title *elder*. This is based on my experience in church life in an organic setting. A lifetime of experience in the arena of organic church life has taught me that since titles today convey that which is *not* of the first century, it is better to leave off the titles.

Today the word elder means *ruler*. Elder means overlord. An *elder* is someone to fear. God's people fear elders. They are the greatest fear factory in the body of Christ. That alone should cause us to abandon the present position of eldering.* The title elder, with its overlording, is just too engraved in our minds. I will add that, next to a pastor, elders are the greatest hindrance to the functioning of the body anywhere on earth today.

Ordinary people who just emerge out of the church's DNA are not feared, nor are they looked upon with awe. They are just brothers and sisters.

Rethinking Elders, SeedSowers Publishing House.

An elder is an elder, without the title. Skip the title and we are all safer for it! Today people change when they get a title . . . and not for the better.

Organic church life will eventually have elders, even without titles. Eldership is just "there."

Calling a man an elder does not make him an elder. Calling a man an evangelist does not make him an evangelist. In the early church, those grew up out of the *daily* outliving of church life.* Everything else is make-believe labeling and evangelical dreaming!

If you must really know who the elders are, then I recommend the following. This may not have a scriptural ground, but it works a lot better than today's very artificial approach.

Ask the women in the church to list, by secret ballot, the three or four brothers in the church whom they trust the most or who are the most caring and thoughtful. Count your ballots. There may be only *one* consistent name, or two, or three. Rarely four. Whatever the results, these are your elders. Not the big, the brash, the outspoken, the feared, or even the respected, but the ones who are naturally the most caring!

Now, get ready for a shock!

Two or three years later, do the same thing over again. *The list of names will have changed . . .* and two more years later, changed again.

I repeat, elders are not forever. Eldership in a church changes! Solidify eldership permanently and you will wreck forever the church's oneness and her creativity and, eventually, perhaps even her existence.

I have a dear friend who tells a lovely story that sheds light on this matter of titles, labels, and manmade offices and ordinations.

---

* Calling a man an apostle surely does not make him an apostle.

CHAPTER TWELVE

THE STORY OF THE HARDBOILED EGG

A mother, Barbara by name, boiled eggs for her children, so that when they came home from school they could have a boiled egg for a snack. To distinguish hard-boiled eggs from the uncooked eggs, Barbara placed an "H" with a marking pen on the eggs that had been hard-boiled.

One day her little son came home, opened the refrigerator, looked for an "H" egg, but saw none; so, he found a marking pen and wrote an "H" on one of the eggs, sat down at the table and started to eat what he believed was now a hard-boiled egg. (After all, the egg had now been labeled "H"; that made it an "H" egg, did it not?) When he cracked open the egg, he discovered that the label had not turned the egg to hard-boiled.

The little boy had not made a mistake any greater than the kingdom of God does when we apply the terms "New Testament church," elders, etc. Crack that label and you will discover it may not be what the label indicated. The label does not make the man.

———— • ————

CHAPTER THIRTEEN

In Our Day, Then, How Shall We Walk?

What are the ingredients necessary for an organic church?

First is the end of the evangelical mind-set.

Get the image of a pastor (and today's minister) out of your mind. If he is there, organic church life will *never* come into being!

Next, at some point, God's people eventually must be left alone. All alone. First they must have help, yes. Then left alone! Maybe six months of help, or a year, and then left alone. Otherwise, there will be no organic church and no real church life.

CHAPTER FOURTEEN

ALBANIA, AN EXAMPLE

It was my privilege to be in Albania when that nation first opened to the world after fifty years of being sealed off from the outside. No one had ever seen the inside of that nation. Upon arriving there, I saw something I had never seen before: Hundreds of missionaries had arrived within hours of the country's opening to the free world. Most of these missionaries were American or British. All had a vision: "Albania is a pure, virgin field; this time we can do it better."

Albanians knew nothing of western Christianity, and they were getting saved by the thousands. Alas, very soon there also appeared church buildings, pulpits, pews, and the entire American Christian practice. That meant Albanians were soon sitting in rows of lined-up chairs and listening in silence to someone preaching. Very simply, there was an American-style church in Albania. There was no way to tell the difference. The two practices were the same. Only the language was different.

So what happened to Christianity in Albania? The American/Albanian churches began dying. In two years the American missionaries were preaching "We need a revival!"

No! Albania needed an organic Albanian church!

I am not ashamed to say I was horrified to see all this taking place. It is a great loss that most Christian workers have never read Roland Allen's *The Spontaneous Church*. A spontaneous church is just possibly the purest, most beautiful experience any Christian could ever know. In the beginning, the Albanian Christians had been enthusiastic about the Lord, but soon they were staying home (a very American Christian trait). Those who did attend church services were developing the same "thou-sand-yard stare" that American Christians display every Sunday morning.

The chance to have an organic church never got even a first breath, and a functioning body of Christ was never born. Pulpits, pews and endless sermons won again!

Albanians were not attending those American-style meetings, and it was because they were bored. Bored with *ritual*—foreign American ritual. And sitting, and sitting!

By contrast, I watched one small group of Christians in Albania with only *two weeks* of help, who, because of circumstances, had been left alone for a year (and even without a New Testament!) While they were on their own, they were experiencing Christ in freedom and in an expression of church life that was 100% Albanian *and* unlike any expression of "church" in Albania or anywhere else on earth.

What were the Albanians in this unusual group told to do from that point on? They had the privilege of being told only to meet with one another, have meals together, talk to the Lord, write some songs using their own Albanian folk music melodies, care for one another, and tell one another about their "this week" touch with Christ.

Some of us had the privilege of watching Albanian Christians *being Albanian Christians*. The only thing they had going for them was the fact they had their own way of relating to the Lord and to one another!

The Albanians came up with a unique way to start their meetings. They all met in Tirana Square and then walked together to the house where they gathered.

The songs they wrote were among the most beautiful I have ever heard, with melodies dating back centuries.

None of them had ever heard the term "Amen." When sharing with one another, they spontaneously responded, "Of course, of course!"

(English translation)

The Albanians *naturally* cared for one another, and were constantly together. They helped one another financially and with finding jobs, and were in every way "one" in all they did.

One brother was bold enough to talk to other people about Christ. (Lo, and behold, an *evangelist*!) There was another brother who was always there to encourage the others when someone in the church was "down" a little. (An exhorter!) They spontaneously decided to go to some towns, and they preached Christ on the street. (No one had ever mentioned to them the idea of doing this!) One brother spoke a little in a few meetings. (They loved it!)

No pastor . . . none . . . nobody!!

This was an expression of the body of Christ in Albania. The meetings "fit" Albanians. It looked Albanian and was natural to Albanians. All they did was spontaneous, natural, and organic. A year later, they were introduced to the New Testament . . . letters written by first-century believers, all bound together under one cover. They could hardly imagine "what luck," and that some of it had been written in Greece, which was their next-door neighbor! They cried when they read about Paul's beatings in the land of Greece.

CHAPTER FIFTEEN

A FOREIGN LAND INSIDE ALBANIA

Albanians have a way of expressing their Albanian culture, but this was not happening for the Christians gathering in Albania under the leadership of missionaries and their foreign traditions.

The culture of every people on earth is different from all other cultures. Eskimos have their way of expressing themselves to other Eskimos, Italians to Italians, and so also Chinese, Hottentots, and Albanians.

And, if you please, even Americans have an American culture.

Was it an *organic American* expression of church life which was given to the Albanians? No, absolutely not. Here is a question: Does America have an organic American expression of the church?

No. America's way of meeting originated in rituals born during the Reformation. Few Americans have ever had the delightful privilege of seeing an organic American expression of the church. Why? Because a spontaneous organic expression of church has rarely happened in this country.

A few brave men are needed who will dare to attempt to discover the organic expression of the church in

America . . . and in every land on earth. These brave men will need to start over from scratch.

Paul had a few words for the church in Corinth which we could well learn from. Paul said that if a neophyte (that is, a new convert or someone who is not even a believer) comes into your meeting in Corinth, he should not feel like he has walked into a foreign country.

The church which the Americans brought to Albania (and other lands) is foreign to the natives. When they walk in, they do not feel "at home." It should be no surprise to us that the Albanians did not like our five-hundred-year-old Reformation ritual which has been retransplanted worldwide. Counterwise, Albanian visitors who came into the "home grown" Albanian meetings immediately sat down and felt at home.

The United States of America also awaits an expression of the church of Jesus Christ that is native and natural to Americans. We have taken American Christianity to the ends of the world, yet what we took to the world is not even *American*! We are fast approaching the point where all evangelical churches on this planet adhere to an American ritual that is natural and organic to *no one*.[*]

So, how shall *we* walk?

First, there must be men and women who forsake the entire evangelical practice of church. Second, these men and women need to be extremely daring and radical.

An organic experience of the church seems impossible for most people. Why? Because such a walk includes "walking out."

The alternative? Status quo boredom!

---

[*] Unless you think the state church of Great Britain in the mid-1500's— with its de-Latinized Roman Catholic meeting, the British Book of Common Prayer and the Sunday morning ritual used in Wittenberg, Germany— was organic to the British.

Boredom by any other name is still boredom. A people who do not function are like statues sitting on benches. A cemetery is still not a good source for finding parts for a living being. Nor does calling something "New Testament" make it New Testament! Gathering up people and giving them titles does not give that people the DNA of the corporate body of Christ.

We have overlooked one of the most important aspects of our faith, the organic church. The church you read about in the New Testament does not give us a static record. We are reading the record of the organic expression of the body of Christ.

Holy men of old sat down and wrote the story of what was growing up organically. Is it possible, even they were surprised to see some of the "ways" of the church as she grew up in different countries and in different cultures? I have a notion that was essentially true in Gentile towns like Colossae. Discovering the ways of the church comes first; then comes the scroll. Men chronicled her ways after the spontaneity had occurred. It was a simple story of Christians getting together, learning to meet under the headship of Jesus Christ. These men of old did not read a recipe taken from a New Testament. They did not gather people in a room and say, "Let us see now, we need elders, so you be an elder," etc. Yet, we come along, pore over those ancient records and say, "Ah, we have to be what they were, so we must be certain we have all these things or we will not be biblical."

The New Testament was not given to us as a fixed or time-static document or documents, with numbered passages which we can paste together. It is a record of a fluid and biological outliving of a dynamic corporate woman and what happened in the first forty years she was on earth (A.D.30-70). It is the story in action of a people who were fallen in flesh but indwelt by divine life in their spirits . . . living one rollercoaster of a ride as they lived and met together under the headship of Jesus Christ!

Nor were any two churches or stories (letters) the same. For example, Corinth is not the story of the church in Thessalonica. The story of what happened in Galatia has little in common with what happened in Colossae or Philippi. Each one of those churches was different—different in makeup, in birth, in language, in customs, circumstances, and problems . . . and definitely different in expression. They were different peoples, all struggling corporately through their unique crises. Consider that each church had different cultures, governments, geo-political situations and laws. But within each culture, each language, each nation, each circumstance, and within the mix of personalities among those cultures, there grew up ways of expressing themselves that were natural to them. They did things which were natural to their place on the map. Each church was different, but each with the DNA of Christ Himself . . . and the natural DNA of Christ's bride.

The organic church is possible. But when you hear "church discipline," or "rebellion," or "submission," head for the door. Your leaders have run out of ideas about what to do with the problems that have arisen.

Another thing you can expect to happen, in many cases when a group of Christians gather together in a home, is that there is someone present who is itching to "teach the New Testament" to others. Ask him or her to first spend a year showing you how to live by an indwelling Lord!

Ask him, for the first year, to speak out of personal experience . . . without quoting a verse of Scripture. If he can, and if what he says to you is the very reality of his life, and if he is kind, then follow him. (Be sure, such a man will *never* be a Bible teacher, per se.)

Let me repeat that statement: Men who know Christ well and know him deeply will *never* be Bible teachers. A man itching to teach the Bible will, wittingly or unwittingly, dispense facts, not Christ; information, not Christ. And it will be found in a *very limited part* of the New Testament. (He does not know that his glimpses of the New Testament are small in scope.) He also thinks that by teaching you the Word, that alone will work some kind of miracle of transformation in you. This is a theory based on "transformation by information."

It does not work.

It never has.

It never will.

Nor is strong foundation the child of Bible study. Only Christ Himself is the strong foundation of the church.

There is still an indwelling Lord. That indwelling Lord can be smothered by the accumulation of biblical facts.

There is still the Holy Spirit. And teaching people what the Scripture says *about* the Holy Spirit is not the Holy Spirit.

The Holy Spirit can bring us to a corporate pursuit of Christ.

CHAPTER SIXTEEN

THE SCARY PART OF BIBLE STUDY

Studying the Bible is not what produces an organic church. Here is the scary part. The day will come when the fellow who is teaching the New Testament begins having problems with you. He does not know how to handle this problem (you). He has also exhausted his best stuff that he teaches from the Bible . . . which he thought would transform you. (He has come to the end of his best knowledge of the New Testament, or at least his information about the New Testament.) Obviously he is not the problem. His conclusion: you are the problem. Then he begins digging up parts of the New Testament which deal with control, submission, authority, and a long list of do's and don'ts, some of which apply to you perfectly! That approach is the death knoll for anything genuine and spontaneous. With such control, the chance of an organic church is outside the realm of possibility. Love cannot live in the presence of legalism. Life cannot continue in the presence of rules.

Lady Ekklesia: Gather! Worker: Show her Christ, and then leave. Let her gather and share her Christ. Leave her alone! Then stand back and watch! You will have to give up thinking of pastor, rituals, today's song book and songs, a special person leading, or anyone leading.

This is starting over, from the ground up. You are no longer manufacturing buggies, but intergalactic space ships. There is not a single part of that buggy in the rocketship, including the buggy whip.

CHAPTER SEVENTEEN

CHARACTERISTICS OF MEN WHO WOULD RESTORE THE ORGANIC CHURCH

These were awesome men who founded those early churches. These amazing men had the nerve to abandon God's people to the Lord. Later, they dropped by the churches they had raised up, in order to help them. And, yes, the churches needed the help they got. They received letters from their church planters. This also helped the churches. What do we do with those letters today? Men turn to those letters and extract some of the most unbelievable legalistic ideas and equally unbelievable rituals.

Today we still need an indwelling Lord. We need spiritual men who will raise up a spiritual church . . . and then leave it to Christ. It takes all these elements working together before we can return to an organic ekklesia.

It takes skill. It takes training. It takes *past experience.* Experience means you have previously been part of an organic church before attempting to lead God's people onto a path that is new to you and unknown to God's people. Of all the times the following statement has ever been made, it is most true here: This is no time or place for amateur hour!

Organic churches come from the hands of men who have previously lived in organic churches. The raising up of an organic expression of the church will throw you back to first-century principles and spiritual living, or you and the church will perish in your own inexperience.

The concept of "previous experience" is something we evangelicals cannot seem to conceptualize.[*]

Medical doctors, facetiously, have a scary saying: "See one, do one . . . then hope!"

We evangelicals have an even scarier idea: "*Imagine* it, try it."

To start a church, you take a living Lord, add a living people, show them how to touch their Lord, daily, and know Him intimately. Tell them you are going to leave them! (Be assured, you will have a very attentive audience.) Give God's people practice at functioning, and encourage them to be creative. Leave them with no rules, no law, and set them free from everything.

Then leave them.

If, a year later, you return and the ekklesia is still there, then know that for one brief moment in your life, you may have built with gold, silver and precious stones. (But do not start bragging until the tenth year!)

You will have at least a glimmer of an organic expression of the church. And, yes, it will be far, far more *New Testament* in character than you will ever have by digging up labels out of the Bible and sticking them on people (or churches) who have not grown up in the nurture and growth of the Holy Spirit and in the freedom of organic, corporate life.

I leave it to you, and to men not yet born who will read these words, to understand, by revelation, that the

---

[*]See *Paul's Way of Training Workers or the Seminary's Way,* SeedSowers Publishing House. All the men Paul trained as church planters had been in church life before being trained and before raising up churches.

ekklesia is a girl, a being, not an it, not an organization, not an institution, but a divine woman, in the midst of a fallen world, who is made up of not-yet-perfect people. She is human as well as divine—a *corporate* human being. And she is not to be left out of this Christian adventure.

I will leave it to your generation, and those yet unborn, to break away totally from all of your present ways of doing church, as well as all your theories about church. It may take you a lifetime of bumbling and muddling through and failing, before the Lord Jesus Christ Himself brings the church to a place where the body of Christ gathers together to touch, to know, to experience, to love Christ and establish an intimate relationship with Him.

Those who have traveled this lonely road which leads to the "how" of an organic church now bequeath to you as much a legacy as possibly can be given, and greatly desire that you not have to start at zero. Yes, you will have to dig hard and long to fully grasp that legacy left for you. Nonetheless, you do not have to start from scratch. You will be able to build upon past discoveries, upon other men's experience, joys, and tears.

All it takes is humility. It takes time. The amount of time is always longer than you imagine or expect. In the name of our Lord, do not start at zero. Men have fought hard for the centrality of Christ and for the organic expression of the church. No, no one is inviting you to become part of "us." (There have been enough such movements.) Others have lived that you might learn from the legacy left to you.

In the meantime, be encouraged to know we have walked this path before you. We have lived in organic church life. We have given a group of people breathtaking declaration of the preeminence of Christ in all things.

41

We have lived what we have experienced: knowing the Lord intimately. We have passed on to people to whom we have ministered Christ the "how" of knowing Christ . . . both individually *and* corporately. We have given them practical helps for how to have church life. Then, we walked out and left them alone—sometimes for a year, and sometimes longer, before returning to give them some help.

If this can happen to us, it can happen to you.

I implore you, sir: Dreams, visions, revelations and new methods will fail if you are not a man saturated with a living experience of Jesus Christ. In other words, you had better know Christ and know Him well.* And you had better know His cross in your own life. And you had better have a revelation of the church that is a driving force within you, because it is going to be a long, long season. For those who lead the way out in a return to the organic church, there will be misunderstandings galore. You are up against two major factors: the way we presently think and the schematic, the ruts, through which our thinking passes.

Here is the rub: This must be lived outside institutionalism, and it must be lived to the hilt. Then it is yours to pass on a yet fuller legacy to those who will surely come after you.

---

*If you have not often heard such words, the reason is simple. We evangelicals have a subconscious feeling that if we just sweat hard enough, we will get things done for God. You will look a long time before you find men standing for the centrality of Christ, in both knowledge and experience.

CHAPTER EIGHTEEN

YOUR FIRST HURDLE

Your first hurdle is simple. If you want to restore the organic church, you have to leave institutional Christianity. If you cannot do that, then please be content to pastor a church in a denomination, one with a good retirement plan.

THIS CAN BE DONE!

At first glance, this whole (first-century) approach to "church" looks like a study in suicide.

Is an organic church really possible?

It is indeed reality. Many Christians can testify: The organic church is a reality. Find those daring souls who were "left on their own." Ask them.

After foundational help is given, a church can be left alone and the organic can emerge. God's people can survive, and even flourish. They will tell you that they have seen first-century elements emerge, naturally, organically.

When they see this happen in their very midst, they are awed (and so shall you be).

A people can make it on their own with a minimum of help, but get clear: It is a kind of help not known anywhere in evangelical circles. The needed *equipment* is not available to workers in the evangelical world, nor is the evangelical mind able to conceive what is needed.

Put it another way: Jesus Christ is still alive. Despite our best efforts to the contrary, He can lead His body! That is, if only Christian workers will step aside and give the church room to grow on its own.

It has been my hope that one day this revelation of the church and of the Lord Jesus Christ would become a widespread practice across the earth . . . even a phenomenon that reaches to all lands.

If you want to be instrumental in restoring the organic church, measure yourself by the following question: Do you still see yourself as one leading such a church? Sir, you have to be one who *hates* permanent leadership.

Never say "It cannot be done." It has been done.

But, be advised: The "New Testament church," minus a living, breathing, daily relationship with Jesus Christ, will be found deficient. Add a slogan like "the Bible plus nothing,"* and you will eventually have legalism. Legalism then brings fear, and fear brings death, ten times out of ten. "Only the Bible" mentality leaves out the number one point of the Bible—a living relationship with Jesus Christ. And that relationship *must* be corporate as well as individual.

You must know Christ well. You must be a man free of egotism and a man free of the evangelical mind, before you even begin!

Just about every starting place you can think of does not work when it comes to birthing the organic church.

If you do not see the following, you have made the single most consistent error of Christian workers throughout the ages: You think that God's people can live the Christian life! They cannot. Nor can you. If you do not understand that simple statement, you have not even begun to know your Lord and His ways.

Our mind says: "Look to the Bible to tell us what to do to live the Christian life, and then go do it." This is a study in ultimate futility. We still need the Holy Spirit; we still need an indwelling Lord. If He who is alive is not added to the Scripture, it is dead letter.

---

*Which means the Bible minus having relationship to an indwelling Lord.

This was, is, and forever shall, be true: Christ alone lives the Christian life!

Most of us who are ministers were taught that simply "preaching the Word" would resolve all the problems of everyone sitting in the congregation. But when death runs out of death, then boredom, rebellion, and disappointment in promises made to us *will* cause reaction (schooling or no schooling). To quell the reaction, the hangman's noose of rules and regulations must soon appear.

No, Sir, we do not begin in these rutted places. We can exhaust our knowledge of the New Testament. We will never exhaust our exploration of Jesus Christ, for such is more than can be done in anyone's lifetime.

When that girl ekklesia comes to know Christ intimately and is then left alone to express her DNA, what is displayed is neither an institution nor an organization, nor does she resemble anything that civilization affords. And when she opens her mouth, she does not quote Scripture, she speaks her Lord! This fact drives fallen angels livid. She is hated above all else, simply because she is not of civilization.

She is a creature who belongs—and came from—realms unseen. She is a living creature with divine attributes. Within her walls—where perhaps only God's eyes can fully see—is a new species. She is a heavenly lady who does not do things the way the fallen creation does.

Fallen man lives out his mutated DNA. We call it civilization, his habitat. The Christian, on the other hand, who is a *new man*, a new human, a new humanity, a new creation, a new species, [*] also has a habitat. Our natural

---

[*] The Greek word is actually "a new species," that is, a biologically unique creation.

habitat is this beautiful lady whom we call ekklesia. This habitat does not look like any other place on earth, and fits the new species perfectly and comfortably. *She* is the place her species naturally gathers. In fact, that gathering place is even called *the assembly*.

This lady, with her parts, *when assembled*, looks like she has the genetics of Jesus Christ.

On her good days, she looks a lot like *Him*! (And like Him, she is not an "it." He is a living being. His bride will be no less.)

When such matters consume you, then you are getting close to holding your nose and jumping into the untreaded waters of an organic body of believers.

CHAPTER TWENTY

THE TIME FACTOR

Take note: Restoration of first motions takes longer than the first motions, far more than the beginning ever did!

First-century believers were not there to learn something new. They had no New Testament to study! What they had was a very active, living Lord indwelling them and a corporate body called "ekklesia" which had never learned to do things the wrong way. They had spontaneous love for one another, which automatically comes out of God's people when they *experience* the Lord Jesus Christ together! (We have had eighteen hundred years learning how to do it the wrong way. We have more to unlearn than they had to learn.)

The breaking down of the present evangelical Christian mindset (because it has been so long with us) is going to take *three hundred* years. Maybe by then, such practices as found here will become commonplace throughout this earth.

Another reason it will take so long: the fall of man!

CHAPTER TWENTY-ONE

THE MOST IMPORTANT ELEMENT OF ALL

The early churches, and the believers within them, were experiencing Christ together. We must lay hold of this one understanding above all else: The organic church is a people together, experiencing Christ together. Out of that flows the *function* of Christ Himself. Otherwise, we are on no more than a journey of imagination leading to a Scripture-quoting wonderland.

What does function mean? In fact, what does the "body of Christ functioning" mean?

The body of Christ is a part of Christ. Long ago, in Galilee, there were certain things Jesus Christ did. Today Christ is carrying out the same functions which He did then. The difference is, it is the *body* part of Christ which is carrying out these functions. This means that when the body functions, it is Christ who is functioning—Christ functioning again through the members. Or, more correctly, when Christ functions, the body of Christ expresses His functions.

All that we have restored, and hope to see restored, can and must, naturally, simply, and *organically,* rise out of the *daily life of Christians experiencing their Lord together.*

It will be a Christ-centeredness to an extent that simply does not exist in today's ever-evolving evangelical land.

I dare not paint a rosy picture, here. Are there problems? More than you can imagine. (But do not forget, solutions to many of those problems are part of the legacy we have left you.) Yes there are problems, but His people go through their trials and tribulations, passing through their corporate crises and their corporate victories, together.

Again, nothing in this book will ever work except there be a living and dynamic *corporate relationship* with Jesus Christ! Further, such church life must come from having received practical, down-to-earth handles for how to know Him intimately. The church must have received practical and spiritual growth from the worker who helped them and then left them.

CHAPTER TWENTY-TWO

My Own Greatest Fear

What you have read here could catch the imagination of an organizational man. God only knows what kind of scheme he (you?) might come up with.

On the other hand, there is solace in knowing he *will* fail.

His plans have one piece missing.

For that one missing piece to be found requires a long and solitary journey into Christ. *That* is a necessity.

You must establish such a walk in *your* own life before you can give it to God's people. This walk must first be the very essence of your daily life.

Many workers will claim such a walk. Few—very, very few—will have it. Fortunately, that fact will come out, sooner or later. It is here, at the necessity of a real and daily walk with Christ, that almost all men draw the line. To live in His presence, to also live crucified, without a murmuring word—virtually all men seem to fall on the short side of that drawn line.

But, oh, there are a small number of men who give up their traditional ministry to learn Christ and to learn Christ in a corporate experience.

Thank God for history's rare exceptions.

CHAPTER TWENTY-THREE

YOUR PART IN RESTORATION

Take the torch: Bring that lady back!

We have a habit of looking at the New Testament and announcing that we need to bring back the power, the miracles, etc. of the first century. What we are doing is looking at only one pea in a peapod. The organic church is a *whole*. She does not overemphasize one part of her nature as over against the neglect of another, nor does she rush to fulfill anything. The organic church is exactly what the word organic implies: a biological being.

What does she lack? Very little. The only thing she needs is some men called of God who will lay aside the present practices and thinking, and will live and die bringing this beautiful lady back to her organic nature.

The torch awaits. It awaits its bearers.

Author Biography

Gene Edwards hold a B.A. from East Texas University, and a B.D. as well as an MDiv. from Southwestern Baptist Theological Seminary (1955), where he graduated at age 22. He is the author of over 30 books; some two million have been printed. His publishers areZondervan, Random House, and Tyndale. His best-known book are *The Divine Romance, A Tale of Three Kings,* and *The Day I Was Crucified, as Told by Jesus Christ.* He pioneered and still belongs to the house church movement. He has been called *America's most loved Christian storyteller.*

During the early years of his ministry, Edwards was a pastor and evangelist. He held city-wide campaigns sponsored by ministerial associations. He has been a frequent guest on Christian television and national Christian radio and a lecturer at seminaries and Bible schools throughout America as well as conference speaker on four continents.

****

To contact the author write to:
gene@geneedwards.com
or
Gene Edwards
PO Box 3450
Jacksonville, FL 32206

ISSUES WE DARE NOT FACE

PAUL'S WAY OF TRAINING WORKERS
OR
THE SEMINARY'S WAY

Take a 2000-year-old journey through *seminary* history. You will discover that the origins of seminaries are not scriptural!

What you read here has never been written in a book, ever.

Why is it important for you to be interested in the seminary's origin and history? It is because ministers are trained in seminaries, which is a concept that, historically, evolved out of pagan education and reflects nothing of the way Jesus and Paul trained men.

You will then discover Paul's way of training workers. This, too, is a subject never before explored.

WHY DID WE PUBLISH THIS BOOK?

To reach men and women called of God, pointing them to a higher and better and far more scriptural way to be trained, and to reveal the *purpose* for being trained. These are issues never before faced.

You will also receive an excerpt from this book to share with others entitled *The Way Paul Trained Workers*. **$14.95**

THE SHOCKING STORY
OF THE
HISTORY OF *BIBLE STUDY*

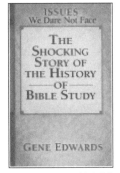

Who would ever think of such a subject. Once engaged, this book is not only shocking, but an eye-opener to the most basic problem in Christendom. We are studying the New Testament in a way that is untenable. This book reveals the wrong way and the best way to study the Scriptures. You may completely change the way you read your Bible, which in turn may change your life as it opens a way you never imagined for reading your Bible.

$14.95

(Originally intended to be entitled *An Introduction to Revolutionary Bible Study*)

(Not the history of the Bible, but the history of Bible study)

ISSUES WE DARE NOT FACE

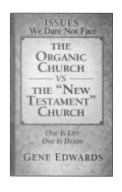

THE ORGANIC CHURCH
VS
THE "NEW TESTAMENT" CHURCH

The most sacred of all cows is now challenged . . . the need of a "New Testament" church. Here is *the* New Testament church, *i.e.* the church that is organic. When the early churches were being formed, there was *no* New Testament in existence. What was emerging were churches which were organic to their very nature. Here is a new wrinkle on the evangelical brain—a totally new, better, and more scriptural way for the church to be born and to grow. The organic church, one that is wonderful, exciting and *natural* to God's people, and totally different to the way churches are raised up in modern times. There is a DNA of the church, and when she is raised up organically, she is a living creature, not a structure—the church spontaneous.

The reason for this book: to bring to us a totally new beginning for the body of Christ. **$9.95**

And Now to
An Issue We Dare NOT Even Think About!!

WHY YOU SHOULD CONSIDER
LEAVING THE PASTORATE

The Catholics must have a pope; we must have a pastor. It took the Reformation to show us that the pope was not in the New Testament.

In the years before the Reformation, the practice of the church's having a pope was *never* questioned. Today the practice of the pastorate is also never questioned. Here is an issue no one ever faces. The function of what a pastor does in carrying out the pastorate has no equivalent in Scripture.

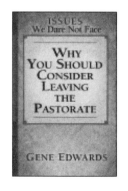

This book does not make that fact the central issue. The issue is the incredible distraction that comes to a Christian called of God who is attempting to carry out this utterly nonscriptural task. Here is a book every pastor should read. It could liberate your life. For just one brief moment, you may want to consider that your call is not that of being called to the pastorate. **$8.95**

HOUSE CHURCH HELPS

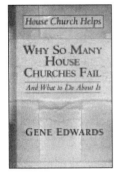

$7.95

WHY SO MANY HOUSE CHURCHES FAIL
AND
WHAT TO DO ABOUT IT

Here are forty years of church life experience that give workable answers. Everyone who has left the institutional church should read this book. The truth is, most house churches do fail. Why? The answer lies in how they begin. The author provides a fresh new departure from the *usual* way house churches begin. He then tells how to have a house church that will last.

PROBLEMS *AND* SOLUTIONS
IN
HOUSE CHURCHES

What are the problems in house churches? Why are Christians ill-equipped to deal with problems? Home churches have problems totally different from other churches. Here in this book you meet the unexpected problems—problems combined with practical solutions . . . which work. There is no theory or dreaming here. These are solutions which have stood the test of time. Expect to discover a whole new world of problems accompanied by solutions as unique and unexpected as the problems themselves.

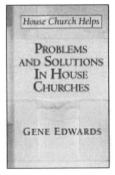

$9.95

HOW TO START A HOUSE CHURCH FROM SCRATCH

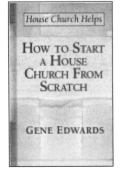

The first house church which was deliberately started in America was started by this author. Others followed. The reason these churches survive is because of the way they began. You will find the reason for their survival—unusual and unheard of—in the content of this audacious book. Everyone with an adventurous heart, looking for unusual answers, will enjoy reading this book.

$8.95

House Church Movement

Beyond Radical
Gene Edwards

What if you found out that little we Protestants practice originates in the first century? The author describes where and how we got our present-day practices. He then calls us to move *Beyond Radical* to see true change in the church.

Read *Beyond Radical* only if you are seeking an alternative to Sunday morning services! This book could make a radical Christian out of you.

$7.⁹⁵

How to Meet in Homes
Gene Edwards

There is a warning from the author on the back of this book. It reads as follows:

This book is for those believers who want to utterly abandon it all, from top to bottom, and then start over in a way that is a revolutionary, radical departure from all present-day practices. $11.⁹⁵

Revolution, the Story of the Early Church
Gene Edwards

A rip-roaring, hair-raising, edge-of-your-seat saga of the first-century believers. From the Day of Pentecost on, through the first seventeen years, every historical figure is there, alive, vivid, believable.

An historical cliffhanger written like a novel. $11.⁹⁵

When the Church Was Led Only by Laymen
Gene Edwards

Edwards clearly reveals that throughout Scripture, it is the brothers and sisters who direct the church.

Discover your birthright . . . to function in a meeting of the body . . . not just sit in a pew as a spectator ! $5.⁰⁰

The First-Century Diaries

by

Gene Edwards

IF YOU NEVER READ ANY OTHER BOOKS ON THE NEW TESTAMENT
. . . READ *THE FIRST-CENTURY DIARIES*!

Here is more than what you would learn
in seminary! The Diaries will revolutionize your
understanding of the New Testament, and, in turn will revolutionize
your life. The best part is, this set of diaries reads like a novel. Never
has learning the New Testament been so much fun.

I.

The Silas Diary

This historical narrative parallels the book of Acts,
giving a first-person account of Paul's first journey.

The Silas Diary is your invitation to join Silas, Paul,
and their companions on a journey fraught with danger and
adventure - a journey that changed the history of the world.
Learn with the first-century Christians what freedom in
Christ really means.

II.

The Titus Diary

This compelling narrative continues the events of the
Book of Acts. *The Titus Diary* is a firsthand account of
Paul's second journey as told by Titus.

Join this journey as Paul sets out once more-this time
with Silas, Timothy, and Luke-and learn of the founding of
the churches in Philippi, Thessalonica, Corinth, and
Ephesus. Look on as Paul meets Aquila and Priscilla and
quickly gains an appreciation of their passion for the Lord
and his church.

The First-Century Diaries

III.

The Timothy Diary

In *The Timothy Diary* Paul's young Christian companion Timothy gives a firsthand account of Paul's third journey.

This journey is quite different from Paul's others. It is the fulfillment of Paul's dream, for in Ephesus Paul trains a handful of young men to take his place after his death. Paul follows Christ's example in choosing and training disciples to spread the gospel and encourage the growth of the church.

IV.

The Priscilla Diary

Here are the stories of Paul's continued travels to the first-century churches narrated from the unique perspective of Priscilla, a vibrant first-century Christian woman!

See Paul writing his most personally revealing letter, his letter to the church in Corinth. Marvel at the truths Paul conveys to the church in Rome, a letter "of all that Paul considered central to the Christian life."

V.

The Gaius Diary

Paul and Nero meet face to face in a moment of highest drama.

Paul is released, but soon is arrested again, and again faces Nero. The sentence is death. Just before his execution, all the men he trained arrived in Rome to be with him. *The Gaius Diary* gives life-changing insight into Paul's final letters. Colossians, Ephesians, Philemon, and Philippians come alive as you see in living color the background to these letters. Be there in April of 70 A.D. when Jerusalem is destroyed.

For the first time ever in all church history, here is the entire first-century story from beginning to end.

The Chronicles of Heaven

by

Gene Edwards

The Old Testament

The Beginning covers *Genesis*, chapters 1&2 (*The Promise* will come next, covering the rest of *Genesis*). *The Escape*, already in print, covers *Exodus*. Other volumes will follow until the Pentateuch is finished.

In *The Beginning* God creates the heavens and the earth. The crowning glory of creation, man and woman, live and move in both the visible world and the spiritual world.

Experience one of the greatest events of human history: *The Escape* of the Israelite people from Egypt. Watch the drama from the view of earthly participants and the view of angels in the heavens.

Experience the wonderful story of the incarnation of Jesus, seen from both realms. *The Birth* introduces the mystery of the Christian life for those who have never heard the story.

The New Testament

The Chronicles then extend into the New Testament. They are *The Birth* and *The Triumph*. After *The Triumph* comes *The First-Century Diaries*!

In *The Triumph* you will experience the Easter story as you never have before. Join angels as they comprehend the suffering and death of Jesus and the mystery of free will in light of God's Eternal Purpose.

The Door has moved to a hill on Patmos. What would John be allowed to see? *The Return* invites you to witness the finale of the stirring conclusion to *The Chronicles of Heaven*.

An Introduction to
The Deeper Christian Life

In Three Volumes
by
Gene Edwards

Living by the Highest Life

If you find yourself unsettled with Christianity as usual . . . if you find yourself longing for a deeper experience of the Christian life . . . *The Highest Life* is for you.

Did Jesus Christ live the Christian life merely by human effort? Or did Jesus understand living by the Spirit—His Father's Life in Him?

Discover what it means to live a spiritual life while living on earth.

I.

The Secret to the Christian Life

Read the Bible, pray, go to church, tithe . . . is this what it means to live the Christian life? Is there more to living the Christian life than following a set of rules? How did Jesus live by the Spirit?

The Secret to the Christian Life reveals the one central secret to living out the Christian life. Nor does the book stop there . . . it also gives *practical* ways to enhance your fellowship with the Lord.

II.

The Inward Journey

The Inward Journey is the companion volume to *The Secret to the Christian Life*. A beautiful story of a dying uncle explaining to his nephew, a new Christian, the ways and mysteries of the cross and of suffering. Of those who have a favorite Gene Edwards book, tens of thousands have selected *The Inward Journey* as that book.

III.

The Divine Romance

by
Gene Edwards

The Divine Romance is praised as one of the all-time literary achievements of the Protestant era. Breathtakingly beautiful, here is the odyssey of Christ's quest for His bride. *The Divine Romance* is the most captivating, heartwarming and inspirational romance, transcending space and time. In all of Christian literature there has never been a description of the crucifixion and resurrection which so rivals the one depicted in *The Divine Romance*.

Many readers have commented, "This book should come with a box of Kleenex." The description of the romance between Adam and Eve alone is one of the great love stories of all times.

Edwards' portrayal of the romance of Christ and His bride takes its place along side such classics as Dante's *The Divine Comedy* and Milton's *Paradise Lost*. Reading this literary masterpiece will alter your life forever.

One of the greatest Christian classics of all time.

THE NEW TESTAMENT
IN FIRST PERSON

THE STORY OF MY LIFE
AS TOLD BY JESUS CHRIST

Listen to Jesus, the Christ, tell His own story. . . in His own words. . . to you !

All four Gospels have been combined in one single, flowing narrative. And it is in the first person! The Story of My Life as Told by Jesus Christ is a complete and thorough account of the events of Christ's life. Now you can read all of the Lord's life in chronological order, without repetition of a single detail. Every sentence in the Gospels is included, plus times, dates and places.

Allow yourself to be immersed into the setting of the life and ministry of Christ. Follow His footsteps as He walked the earth with those He knew and loved, in one smooth, flowing, uninterrupted story.

The impact is so arresting you will feel that you are hearing the gospel story for the first time. And always, in first person, the Lord is speaking directly to you. Think of it as The Jesus Diary.

ACTS IN FIRST PERSON

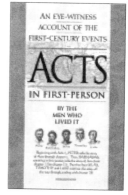

For the first time in history, you can read the Acts of the Apostles in first person . . . like a diary.

Listen to the men who lived during the exciting early years of the church. Experience the excitement and danger as these men travel to declare Jesus Christ. Every detail is included . . . such as dates and location.

Based on Tyndale's New Living Translation Bible, *Acts in First Person* is in readable, contemporary English. A wonderful study aid for all ages.

SEEDSOWERS
800-228-2665   (fax) 866-252-5504
www.seedsowers.com

REVOLUTIONARY BOOKS ON CHURCH LIFE

Beyond Radical *(Edwards)* 7.95
How to Meet in Homes (*Edwards*) 10.95
An Open Letter to House Church Leaders (*Edwards*) 5.00
When the Church Was Led Only by Laymen *(Edwards)* 5.00
Revolution, The Story of the Early Church (*Edwards*) 11.95
The Silas Diary (*Edwards*) 9.99
The Titus Diary (*Edwards*) 8.99
The Timothy Diary (*Edwards*) 9.99
The Priscilla Diary (*Edwards*) 9.99
The Gaius Diary *(Edwards)* 10.99
Overlooked Christianity (*Edwards*) 10.95
Paul's Way of Training Workers or the Seminary's Way (*Edwards*) 14.95
The Shocking Story of the History of Bible Study (*Edwards*) 14.95
Why You Should Consider Leaving the Pastorate (*Edwards*) 8.95
The Organic Church vs. the "New Testament" Church (*Edwards*) 9.95
Problems and Solutions in House Churches (*Edwards*) 9.95
How to Start a House Church from Scratch (*Edwards*) 8.95
Why So Many House Churches Fail and What to Do about It (*Edwards*) 7.95

AN INTRODUCTION TO THE DEEPER CHRISTIAN LIFE

Living by the Highest Life (*Edwards*) 10.99
The Secret to the Christian Life (*Edwards*) 9.99
The Inward Journey (*Edwards*) 10.99

CLASSICS ON THE DEEPER CHRISTIAN LIFE

Experiencing the Depths of Jesus Christ (*Guyon*) 9.95
Practicing His Presence (*Lawrence/Laubach*) 9.95
The Spiritual Guide (*Molinos*) 9.95
Union with God (*Guyon*) 8.95
The Seeking Heart (*Fenelon*) 9.95
Intimacy with Christ (*Guyon*) 10.95
Spiritual Torrents (*Guyon*) 10.95
The Ultimate Intention (*Fromke*) 10.00
One Hundred Days in the Secret Place *(Edwards)* 12.99

IN A CLASS BY ITSELF

The Divine Romance (*Edwards*) 11.99

NEW TESTAMENT

The Story of My Life as Told by Jesus Christ *(Four Gospels blended)* 14.95
The Day I was Crucified as Told by Jesus the Christ 14.99
Acts in First Person *(Book of Acts)* 9.95

COMMENTARIES BY JEANNE GUYON

Genesis 10.95
Exodus 10.95
Leviticus - Numbers - Deuteronomy 12.95
Judges 7.95
Job 10.95
Song of Songs *(Song of Solomon Commentary)* 9.95

(Prices subject to change)

COMMENTARIES BY JEANNE GUYON *(Continued)*

Jeremiah Commentary 7.95
James - I John - Revelation Commentaries 12.95

THE CHRONICLES OF HEAVEN *(Edwards)*

Christ Before Creation 8.99
The Beginning 8.99
The Escape 8.99
The Birth 8.99
The Triumph 8.99
The Return 8.99

THE COLLECTED WORKS OF T. AUSTIN-SPARKS

The Centrality of Jesus Christ 19.95
The House of God 29.95
Ministry 29.95
Service 19.95
Spiritual Foundations 29.95
The Things of the Spirit 10.95
Prayer 14.95
The On-High Calling 10.95
Rivers of Living Water 8.95
The Power of His Resurrection 8.95

COMFORT AND HEALING

A Tale of Three Kings *(Edwards)* 8.99
The Prisoner in the Third Cell *(Edwards)* 9.99
Letters to a Devastated Christian *(Edwards)* 7.95
Exquisite Agony *(Edwards)* 9.95
Dear Lillian *(Edwards) paperback* 5.95
Dear Lillian *(Edwards) hardcover* 9.99

OTHER BOOKS ON CHURCH LIFE

Climb the Highest Mountain *(Edwards)* 12.95
The Torch of the Testimony *(Kennedy)* 14.95
The Passing of the Torch *(Chen)* 9.95
Going to Church in the First Century *(Banks)* 5.95
When the Church Was Young *(Loosley)* 8.95
Church Unity *(Litzman,Nee,Edwards)* 10.95
Let's Return to Christian Unity *(Kurosaki)* 10.95

CHRISTIAN LIVING

The Christian Woman . . . Set Free *(Edwards)* 12.95
Your Lord Is a Blue Collar Worker *(Edwards)* 7.95
The Autobiography of Jeanne Guyon 19.95
Final Steps in Christian Maturity *(Guyon)* 12.95
Turkeys and Eagles *(Lord)* 9.95
The Life of Jeanne Guyon *(T.C. Upham)* 17.95
Life's Ultimate Privilege *(Fromke)* 10.00
Unto Full Stature *(Fromke)* 10.00
All and Only *(Kilpatrick)* 8.95
Adoration *(Kilpatrick)* 9.95
Release of the Spirit *(Nee)* 9.99
Bone of His Bone *(Huegel) modernized* 9.95
You Can Witness with Confidence *(Rinker)* 10.95